**CLARINET**

FOR THE BEGINNER

**AMY ADAM**
**MIKE HANNICKEL**

T0057437

Speed • Pitch • Balance • Loop

To access audio visit:
**www.halleonard.com/mylibrary**
Enter Code
6766-6527-4107-9915

ISBN 978-90-431-1696-1

Visit Hal Leonard Online at
**www.halleonard.com**

Contact us:
**Hal Leonard**
7777 West Bluemound Road
Milwaukee, WI 53213
Email: info@halleonard.com

In Europe, contact:
**Hal Leonard Europe Limited**
42 Wigmore Street
Marylebone, London, W1U 2RN
Email: info@halleonardeurope.com

In Australia, contact:
**Hal Leonard Australia Pty. Ltd.**
4 Lentara Court
Cheltenham, Victoria, 3192 Australia
Email: info@halleonard.com.au

**Amy Adam, Mike Hannickel**

**TONS OF TUNES for the Beginner**

**Clarinet**

**ISBN 90-431-1696-3**

Audio arrangements by James L. Hosay

# ARRANGERS

**MIKE HANNICKEL** grew up in the Sacramento, California area and attended California State University, Sacramento and the University of Southern California. He has been a music teacher in Rocklin, California since 1973. He also composes and publishes exclusively with Curnow Music Press with whom he has dozens of pieces of music in print.

**AMY ADAM** was raised in Grand Rapids, Minnesota and attended the University of Minnesota, Duluth graduating with a BM in band education and Flute performance. She has been a music teacher in California since 1992 and currently teaches in Rocklin, California.

# TONS OF TUNES

**TONS OF TUNES FOR THE BEGINNER** is filled with the fun and familiar tunes that beginners love to play. All the songs have been arranged in keys that beginning band students learn in every popular band method. All **TONS OF TUNES FOR THE BEGINNER** books can be used together.

The **professional quality accompaniment recordings** can be used for practice and performance. You may also choose to purchase the separately available Piano accompaniment part.

The songs are in **carefully graded** order. You will find appropriate music for every level of early beginner.

### TO THE TEACHER:

*For private studio teachers:* **TONS OF TUNES FOR THE BEGINNER** is an excellent and versatile choice for use in those early recitals. You can also encourage your students to put on concerts at home for friends and family using the included recordings.

*For band directors:* Motivate your students with these fun and easy songs! **TONS OF TUNES FOR THE BEGINNER** is designed so that any group of band instruments can play together. If, for instance, you have a beginning Flute, Alto Saxophone and Tuba player who would like to perform a piece together, you'll find what you need in this series.

**Spotlight deserving young players in concert** by including music featuring a soloist or small group. This also gives the band some needed rest.

### TO THE MUSICIAN:

Have **FUN** playing these songs alone or with your friends! Even if you have different instruments, you can still play together. Each person needs to get the **TONS OF TUNES FOR THE BEGINNER** book for their instrument.

# CONTENTS

# TONS OF TUNES FOR THE BEGINNER

**Amy Adam** and
**Mike Hannickel** (ASCAP)

## 1. Mary Had a Little Lamb

## 2. Lightly Row

# 3. London Bridge

# 4. Twinkle Twinkle Little Star

# 5. Frere Jacques

# 6. The Party Song

# 7. Yankee Doodle

# 8. This Old Man

# 9. Aura Lee

# 10. The Snake Charmer Song

# 11. Bingo

# 12. Old MacDonald

# 13. When the Saints Go Marching In

# 14. Ode To Joy

# 15. Faith Of Our Fathers

# 16. Crusader's Hymn

# 17. Shoo Fly, Don't Bother Me

# 18. The Can Can

# 19. Mexican Hat Dance

13

# 20. Kum-Bah-Yah

14

# 21. Michael Row the Boat Ashore

# 22. Oh Susannah

15

# 23. For He's a Jolly Good Fellow

# 24. Polly Wolly Doodle

# 25. Pep Band Riff

# 26. Alouette

# 27. Skip To My Lou

# 28. I've Been Working On the Railroad

# 29. Here Comes the Bride

# 30. Amazing Grace

## 31. Grandfather's Clock

# 32. Take Me Out To the Ballgame